Finding Your Authentic Self

Romans 12 Living

R.J. Speelman

Finding Your Authentic Self: Romans 12 Living
Copyright © 2020 by R.J. Speelman

All rights reserved. No part of this book may be reproduced or transmitted in any form or by any means without written permission from the author, except in brief quotations embodied in critical articles or reviews.

All Scripture quotes are taken from the New King James Version.

ISBN (978-1-7345703-0-4)

Photographs by R.J. Speelman
Printed in the United States of America

R.J. Speelman
romans12living.com

DEDICATION

I have no doubt that my life story would be completely different if God was not part of it. Though I have been a Christian for many years, I believe my trust in God is something that blossomed this past year. When my time on this earth is complete, I pray God will consider it one of His masterpieces. God chose me to fulfill a specific purpose and this book is written because I chose to follow that purpose.

I thank my family for being supportive of my many dreams yet recognizing God's hand in all of them. I would never have made it through all of this without my husband and amazing children. I dedicate this book to them; thank you for loving me unconditionally! I am truly blessed!

Table of Contents

Preface 7
Introduction 11
Finding Yourself in Today's World 13
Making Choices, Choosing God 29
What Do You Value? 49
Serving Others, Serving God 67
When in Doubt, Ask God 85
Time for a Relationship with God 105

Preface

If you had asked me a year and a half ago about the content of this book, I would have said I had no idea that the book would even exist. It was not on my heart, in my head, or even part of my day-to-day living. I was working to find balance with my family, my career, and my ailing health. I was certainly not feeling called by God to write! However, as you will find, my life changed in miraculous ways.

Honestly, I didn't want to follow any other path, unless I was the one controlling it. I remember saying to my doctor, "Just give me time…a few more weeks until I have it all planned the way that I think works best." I mean that is how I accomplished all of my dreams in my life, right? It was <u>all about me</u>, research and planning, counting on <u>MY inner drive, passion, gifts, and perseverance</u>!

On that day in November as my career came to an abrupt halt, little did I know that my struggles would become inspirational writings in a book. What started as mentally disorganized thoughts with disjointed sentences and incoherent words evolved into Romans 12 Living. God called me to let go of those things I was focused intently on controlling. Letting go of the essence of myself and my identity, my life's work. For so many people, including myself, my career ~~is~~ was my identity. My heart, my passion, my purpose! I ~~am~~ was so proud of what I ~~have~~ had accomplished in my professional career. (Note: the strikethroughs are on purpose. My perspective has changed.)

One day, about five months after that day in November, I felt a strange sense of what others may call a change of heart. After being continually bombarded with my health issues, I just needed to let go and rest my mind and body. One afternoon I was so exhausted; I couldn't focus, my physical balance was off, and I felt like my body and mind needed to re-boot. It was at that time, a sense of urgency and freedom collided within me. In that moment I was forced into a decision of change, at a time I was not able to control. It was another reminder that God is always in control!

When I realized I would no longer be able to have the career I once did, I was terrified. Wait, what?! It was what defined me; it was my identity. Really? At that same point of panic/angst, something new happened. A simple life of care and compassion, organization and silence called my name. After a very small mind battle (which I still don't understand why I didn't feel the need to fight it), I felt a sense of peace and freedom. You see, it was as if I recognized and accepted that my purpose was now going to be God's purpose. I realized my identity no longer had to be what it was prior to me becoming so ill. I accepted that I would no longer be recognized based on status, a title, or accolades received that at one time I felt defined me.

There is a new identity awaiting me, one where I will find freedom and purpose on a different path; one led by God. My heart, my passion, and my purpose are now focused on what He has planned for me, even without knowing every single detail and time.

Along the way, I realize I will be letting go of material things to follow this new purpose! I am letting go of connections to acquaintances and friends, and no longer attempting to fit in with certain groups of people. (Looking back, I was not really fond of being connected with most of those groups anyway. They were headed in a direction I did not want to follow; it seems that ship had changed its course a while ago.)

Learning to let go of worry and anxiety, self-doubt and judgment, a muted voice, and a controlling environment have been such a blessing. The sense of living simply never sounded enticing to me, but I now can enjoy the simple pleasures of this glorious world and a freedom to explore it. It is like a gate to a lovely place has been opened for me. I believe letting go will lead me to places of tremendous value. Only time will tell…but I trust in God with all of my mind, body, and spirit.

I am on a journey of healing and faith. Yes, I am still fighting my battles. I am often exhausted and broken, yet I am still persevering. Give up, no way! I can't and won't! Do you know why? Not because I am in control, but because God is in control! He is my strength, my rock, my God! To God be all the glory!

"Grace to you and peace from our God the Father and our Lord Jesus Christ, who gave Himself for our sins, that He might deliver us from this present evil age, according to the will of our God and Father, to whom be glory forever and ever. Amen."

~ Galatians 1:3-5

Introduction

"WHATEVER IT TAKES!" Whenever I hear or say these three words, they have a distinctly different meaning today. I realize that "whatever it takes" is really coming to understand God's grace and sovereign power and choosing to follow Him. God is in control! He does "whatever it takes" for us; we just need to make the choice to listen to and follow Him.

Join me on a journey to (and through) places you may or may not have traveled in your life and in your faith with this book as your inspiration. My hope is that you gain some insight through my stories and shared experiences, reflecting on your own life and finding that God indeed has a plan for you. You may not recognize it today, but it will happen! Prepare yourself for God's abundant love and transformation! We are to do "whatever it takes" to follow God and His teachings! We are called to be willing followers, fulfilling God's plans for us here on earth. As you read through each segment of this book, take the time to ponder what is written, pray about what is on your heart, and study the shared Bible verses with others, if possible. You could use this book as a study group text or use it independently. Carve out at least fifteen minutes to read, re-start/regain, and re-focus your conversations with God.

After hours of searching for a specific Bible verse that I felt captured everything I was being called to do with my writing, God surprised me (as usual) with not just a verse, but an entire chapter from the New Testament. Hence, the sub-title and my ongoing web presence, Romans 12 Living.

I am still very much a student of God's Word, but I fervently believe that Chapter 12 from the Book of Romans is calling me to do "whatever it takes" to lead a Christian life. I chose the New King James Version as it is my personal favorite. Of course, my book references many other Books of the Bible, so you will see a wide variety of scriptures shared within my writing.

I hope you walk closer to God as you read my book…
finding your authentic self!

*Finding Yourself
in
Today's World*

"I will praise you, for I am fearfully and wonderfully made; Marvelous are Your works, and that my soul knows very well."

~ Psalms 139:14

Life-Long Learning

What is the most important thing you have learned in your life? Where did you learn it? In school? From a coach? Your parents? A decision you made? An event that happened in your life?

As a life-long educator, I am a huge advocate for learning. However, I believe learning must have <u>authentic value and application</u> if it is to make a lasting impact on our lives. Without these two critical elements, learning becomes a superficial speck of information that is quickly lost from our minds.

For whatever things were written before were written for our learning, that we through the patience and comfort of the Scriptures might have hope.
~ Romans 15:4

This means that God's Word is meant for us to interact with, learn from, and share with others to change the world. It is authentic and is applicable to our daily lives.

As with all true learning, we must gain basic knowledge first, so we can comprehend what it being taught. We are then able to apply what we comprehend, analyzing and reflecting on its value. This is when true understanding happens for us. If we take time to study God's Word, apply it to our lives and reflect on its meaning, then we will see God's Word come alive.

Ponder Point:

God's Word has such authentic value and application in our daily lives. Ask for help as you journey in God's Word. Take time as you use this book to build a better understanding of your relationship with God. You can easily do this alone, journaling in the "A Place to Ponder and Pray" sections. Build in quality time to read Scripture, pray, and search your own soul for a deeper understanding of yourself. In addition, you might find a Bible study group that is a good fit for you or ask others to join you with this book. There are plenty of Christians waiting to meet you! Begin your life-long learning journey today!

Finding Balance

Finding balance in life is not easy! We struggle to find balance between work and play, career and family, marriage and children, service and worship!

I've willingly worked 60+ hours a week, happily pursued and attained academic degrees, served others with joy, worked multiple jobs at one time, skipped sleep to gain time to do one more thing, juggled my career and family roles, but I learned that without balance, I fall down. God loves us and He helps us back up, but we often don't acknowledge Him, and we go right back to what we were doing. We don't recognize the need for balance! We focus right back on end goals, anxiety, and deadlines looming ahead of us.

It doesn't matter if we are serving others (even if it is God's purpose), an unbalanced life will lead us to fall.

"Now it happened as they went that He entered a certain village; and a certain woman named Martha welcomed Him into her house. And she had a sister called Mary, who also sat at Jesus' feet and heard His word. But Martha was distracted with much serving, and she

approached Him and said, "Lord, do You not care that my sister has left me to serve alone? Therefore, tell her to help me." And Jesus answered and said to her, "Martha, Martha, you are worried and troubled about many things. But one thing is needed, and Mary has chosen that good part, which will not be taken away from her."

~ **Luke 10:38-42**

Martha asked Jesus to correct Mary because she chose to stop serving others to listen to Him. Martha was upset and confused (as was I), as she was always overwhelmed with things to do and places to go, when in reality, she needed to find balance.

Do you struggle to choose to make time to be with Jesus, study and listen to the Word, and worship Him? Prioritize what is most important. Remember why balance matters!

Ponder Point:

- Quality is better than quantity.
- Time is more valuable than money!
- Worship God so you can serve others with His Word!
- Serving others should not take away from time spent with God!

Spiritual Authenticity

Integrity and character are not easily found in our world today. Unfortunately, we live in a "me-centered" world, where people say and do things to get what they want at the expense of honesty and kindness. Emotions change quickly and people's motives shift. Of course, integrity and character have never been a 100% guarantee at any point in history.

Making Godly choices based on integrity and character can even lead to losing things for which we faithfully pray. We may have placed our trust in God and fought hard to not worry about what could happen…and yet it still happens! We end up disappointed and emotionally broken. Even in those dark moments, I hope you remember to be true to who you are and what you have been taught. Integrity and character can never be sold nor bought. Remember, God has a plan for us. We need to become who He has called us to be!

We must always recognize our true identity is never hiding from God or ourselves. If we take time to reflect on what is happening around us, we will see the truth.

"As in water face reflects face, so a man's heart reveals the man."

~ **Proverbs 27:19**

Ponder Point:

Life can be cruel! Social conformity is constantly pressuring us to make decisions that can strip our confidence, identity, and character. Be strong, have faith; God is with you! Don't let others disappoint or deceive you.

You are good enough; your identity lies in Christ, not in your circle of friends. Follow what is good; follow God. Let your heart reveal the true you!

BE THE PERSON GOD HAS CALLED

YOU TO BE…

<u>LEAD WITH SPIRITUAL AUTHENTICITY!</u>

Step by Step

We wake up each day with a plan, a desire for what we want to happen and/or what we feel needs to happen for us to be happy. Remember, the Lord wants us to walk with Him, yet He does not force our steps. He allows us to choose to follow our own plan, but step-by step, it is going to be much more difficult than if we would follow His path.

Do you know someone who seems content with what is happening in their life? Have you ever wondered why they seem so balanced and content? Could the difference be that they are listening and following the path God laid out for them to travel? Could they have already learned it is better to trust God and follow the steps He directs because they did their own thing and tried to go their own way first?

Everyone's journey may look different, but God's goal is that everyone gets to the same final destination through salvation! If you meet someone who chose to go their own way first only to recognize God's plan was better, talk with them about their journey. They may tell you how stubborn or lost they really were at that time. Often times, you hear these stories from those we consider old and wise. Seek out their wisdom!

"There are many plans in a man's heart, nevertheless the Lord's Counsel…that will stand."

~ **Proverbs 19:21**

Ponder Point:

Life is full of experiences that help us in our walk with God. Step by step, we come to realize His true plans for our life. It may not be what we want in the moment, but looking back over a lifetime, it is exactly what we needed to happen! Life is a journey of many steps; make a choice to walk it with God!

Your True Self

Do you ever feel like you hide your "true self" from others? Maybe not those immediately close to you, but most people aren't aware of your true thoughts or opinions. At times, many of us feel as if we are living two lives. One of social conformity and the other of spiritual authenticity. Personally, I struggle with caring too much about what others will think or say about my own words or actions as I follow God. What if I don't conform to the norm? What if others find out who I truly am? What will happen?

It is not always going to be easy to follow your true God-given purpose, especially when it might not align with what the rest of the world thinks of you. In the beginning of following God's purpose, you may not even be sure it is the "right thing" to do. Don't let doubt or fear stop you.

I have been in pursuit of social conformity with the world AND attempting to balance spiritual authenticity with God for many years. When my recent illness physically and mentally weakened me, I became spiritually strengthened to lead with authenticity. I longed for the feeling of being whole, not split into two parts. It is a true blessing.

I do not believe I am alone on this journey. Yes, there are people more concerned about social conformity rather than spiritual authenticity. Media encourages everyone to accept and support the social norm and condemns those who try to lead anyone away from social conformity, especially when tied to one's faith in God.

Be strong and lead with spiritual authenticity. Do not fear the world's view of you.

"If God is for us, who can stand against us?"
~ **Romans 8:31**

Ponder Point:

What concerns you most about living in today's world of social conformity? God's Word will strengthen you to do the right thing! Pray and know that God is with you…always!

Are You Ready?

Are you ready for today? Tomorrow? Next week? Do you have everything planned? Lots of people are thinking along those lines when asked the question, but what does it mean to be ready?

Is it something we visually plan and prepare for with a to-do list or planner? I often think about why traveling is so stressful. My family loves to take trips and I plan well ahead of time with a check-off list of things to pack in our luggage. We certainly cannot afford to forget anything, especially with our son's numerous allergies. We do not want to miss our flight since our food supply for him is so limited.

Does being ready always have to do with material preparation? What about mental preparedness? Once you take your seat on that plane, then what? Here is another example…when we sit down to take a test, are we confident we completed our assignments and studied the correct materials? Preparation is expected! If not, it makes us feel stressed and frustrated because we know we will not be able to do our absolute best work.

Yet, no matter how much we can plan, we cannot be prepared for everything. So, then what happens? Are we able to get ready for the unexpected, the unplanned? Have faith and resilience at all times. Even if you are knocked down, no matter what, you are a child of God!
He will take care of you!

"That if you confess with your mouth the Lord Jesus and believe in heart that God has raised Him from the dead, you will be saved."
~ **Romans 10:9**

Ponder Point:

We cannot be prepared for everything, no matter how much we try. We just need to be ready for what God has planned, willing to take action as needed or quietly accept what happens. Pray often and trust God! He will find a way, no matter what!

Then and Now

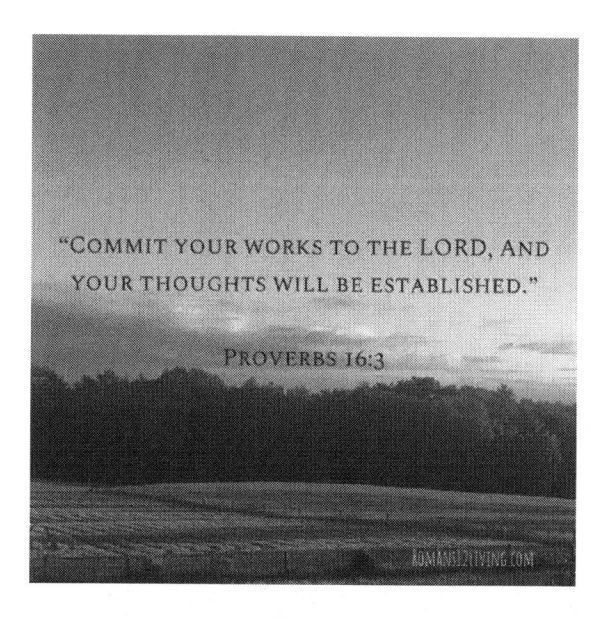

> "COMMIT YOUR WORKS TO THE LORD, AND YOUR THOUGHTS WILL BE ESTABLISHED."
>
> PROVERBS 16:3

Where is your place in this world? Do you want to make your mark on it, build a legacy, or positively impact others? Honestly, all of these have been my goal; it is what drives me forward. There are times I recognize my past goals/accomplishments do not match God's future purpose for me. Yet, I believe my past helped prepare me for the future.

All of us are uniquely gifted by God. Some people call it potential. We also have been given our own free will. With that comes great responsibility. Make your mark on this world with Christ by your side! Let God guide the way with what is yet to come for you!

"Now faith is the substance of things hoped for, the evidence of things not seen."
~ **Hebrews 11:1**

Ponder Point:

God allows us to live our dreams, but it is now time for us to listen to His plans! Are you ready?

Is it possible that all of your past experiences were preparing you for a new identity? God will provide all you need to go on this journey. Make the choice to ask God for guidance! Trust in Him…now and always!

Making Choices, Choosing God

"And if it seems evil to you to serve the Lord, choose for yourselves this day whom you will serve, whether the gods which your fathers served that were on the other side of the River, or the gods of the Amorites, in who land you dwell. But as for me and my house, we will serve the Lord."
~ Joshua 24:15

Follow Him

> "IN ALL YOUR WAYS ACKNOWLEDGE HIM, AND HE SHALL DIRECT YOUR PATHS."
>
> PROVERBS 3:6
>
> ROMANS12LIVING.COM

Check out the marks on the sand in the picture on this page. These are the marks of a giant, female sea turtle coming into a beach in Florida to lay her eggs. It is amazing for me to not only find these tracks, but to know that the female turtle was returning to the place where her life began as a new hatchling. And…her hatchlings will also find their way back to the ocean the same way, returning to the same place themselves when they are old enough to lay eggs. This deep-seeded instinct to continue with the plans of the past is something we all could learn to follow.

Unfortunately, there are a few hatchlings that head the opposite direction each year. They never survive on that path. As they head the other direction, away from the ocean, they are devoured by other animals and the elements! The ocean is their only option to survive and remain alive.

We are not much different. You see, many of us often want to go our own way, to do our own thing. We may hope that God will meet us where we are. Sometimes before we make it back, other things happen. and we are destroyed by the elements and cannot survive. We need our path to lead to our living water; we need Jesus Christ!

"Jesus said to him, "I am the way, the truth, and the life. No one comes to the Father except through Me."
~ **John 14:6**

Follow Him! If we listen and acknowledge Him in all our ways, He is waiting to guide us.

A Different Perspective

Are you patient? Do you wait to hear God's voice before making decisions? We need to pray and patiently wait to hear His response. Do you find you become impatient with your own timeline or that of others, including God? Don't get me wrong; we must all be responsible and meet deadlines, but sometimes we take it too far.

As a past hyper-drive planner, I was compelled to do whatever was needed to accomplish what I had committed myself to doing. Times are different for me now. I encourage you to step back and look at where you are going and where you just came from before deciding to commit to another decision. Isn't that a different perspective?

Ask yourself: ***Is my journey congruent with my purpose?*** This is where learning to be patient and not so strong-willed comes into play! Reflect on what may or may not have worked in the past. We should still set goals, but we need to pray upon those goals, giving God time to teach us some patience…and to gain perspective on our ultimate decisions. It is never too late to make a U-turn.

Thus, says the Lord: "Stand in the ways and see, And ask for the old paths, where the good way is, and walk in it; Then you will find rest for your souls."
~ Jeremiah 6:16

We live in such a fast-paced world today, where patience seems to make us lose our edge in competition. You might fall behind the crowd. Just remember, oftentimes, the crowd is headed in the wrong direction, with stumbling blocks along the way. When others are just blindly following a person or event with rabid emotion and without purposeful thought, do not join them. Stop to reflect, pray, and gain perspective. Ask God for guidance. Walk with Him to find clarity!

Ponder Point:

Patience and perspective are two things we need to focus on more often each day. Patience and perspective will lead to greater contentment with our job/career, our relationships with others, and our own self-worth.

Decisions to lead or follow are ever so important. Patience to discern what is right rather than what is easy is key. Pray each day for patience and perspective!

A Change of Plans

No one looks forward to having plans change. We like to do things on <u>our</u> preferred timeline, which often means *<u>right now</u>*! If you ever experienced a delay at the airport, you know exactly what it means to have your plans changed. Personally, delays at the airport now seem small compared to the medical leave my doctor reported as immediate and necessary. I wanted a delay, but sometimes you get the *<u>right now</u>* response.

Focus on letting God take control of your timeline and watch as things work more smoothly. It may test your faith, but it produces amazing results. Just be <u>prepared to not have</u> solid answers based on some self-created timeline. Instead, watch as your faith is strengthened even while you experience a sense of the unknown. Why? God will slow you down, allowing you to take note of things you would never be able to see in your hurried state of living. Stop rushing past the beauty of His World and observe the blessing of family and friends.

"Have I not commanded you? Be strong and of good courage; do not be afraid, nor be dismayed, for the Lord your God is with you wherever you go."

~ Joshua 1:9

Ponder Point:

You may continue to desire to know where you are headed and what is coming next. Relax and allow your faith in God to create patience as you wait. Enjoy the 'now' moments. If you miss them, you won't get them back! Each day is a gift! Remember to enjoy it, no matter what changes may occur!

Difficult Decisions

As we make difficult decisions in our lives, we may not be thinking about God's Law. We may be thinking about how the decisions we make will impact our finances, our relationships, and our own happiness. Keep this in mind:

"The law of Your mouth is better to me than thousands of coins of gold and silver."
                                                              ~ Psalm 119:72

If we deeply reflect on just this verse, it is saying that we can delight in completely committing ourselves to God's Law rather than pursuing material wealth. (This can be a struggle, especially with a family to support and a standard of living to maintain.)

What will you decide to do? Before you make any decision, use the Bible to find your answers! Take a few moments to check out the verses surrounding Psalm 119:72. They will help you find strength in the decisions you make, no matter how difficult.

Remember, as you are faced with tough decisions:

- Pray to God!
  "Teach me good judgment and knowledge."
  ~ Psalm 119:66

- Acknowledge your past mistakes but focus on making good decisions today.
  "Before I was afflicted, I went astray, but
  now I keep Your word."
  ~ Psalm 119:67

- Stand strong with God's truth as you face social pressures.
  "The proud have forged a lie against me,
  But I will keep Your precepts with my whole heart."
  ~ Psalm 119:6

Heart Decisions

As much as you may want to impact others in a positive way, their mindset is something you cannot control. You may be persuasive and logical, share Biblical evidence, and employ strategies so others might easily connect to experiences. However, if they have no desire to connect, to change or to listen, our efforts fall on deaf ears.

Words written on a page or said to someone who feels that they are doing 'just fine' with themselves, their situation, and their decisions will make little to no impact. A person cannot relate to the words because they do not seem valuable to them in that moment.

> *"The way of a fool is right in his own eyes..."*
> **~ Proverbs 12:15**

No matter how hard we may try, we can only do so much. A person must be willing to listen. Even with that said, be prepared and be resilient in your pursuit of others. Oftentimes, they will want to argue or put down what you share. They may twist what you are attempting to do from something good, turning it into something spiteful and hurtful.

There is an old adage that says, "You can lead a horse to water, but you cannot make it drink." ...Or to apply it to today's writing, "You can lead a person to Scripture, but you cannot force them how to think."

Does this mean we stop offering them water or the Word of God? Not at all; it just means that we must be prepared for what doesn't happen at that moment. It may happen at a later time.

Ponder Point:

Remember, heart decisions are made by each person individually! It can take time, but eventually they will become thirsty for water and start to think about the Word shared with them. When their viewpoint changes, so may their heart's decision. Never give up sharing God's Word!

Growing Up

Do you ever have days or moments when you think back to how you behaved in your younger years as a child? Were you free from responsibilities or did you just choose not to be responsible? Did you say and do things that were impulsive without any real idea of the consequence? Was your lack of knowledge and experience a good thing or not? When did you do the most childish things? Was it yesterday?

"When I was a child, I spoke as a child, I understood as a child, I thought as a child; but when I became a man, I put away childish things."

~ **1 Corinthians 13:11**

You can look at this verse from two perspectives:

- A child truly being young by age, OR
- A person, no matter their age, growing in their journey of Christian faith!

I will be honest, when I was younger in years AND faith, I expected anyone who claimed to be a Christian to walk and talk with poise, never take a misstep in their faith or decisions…essentially I expected those who claimed to be truly devoted followers of Christ to be better than everyone else. It was difficult to see someone I knew who was claiming to be 'all-in' with Christ, making what I considered ungodly decisions one day and exalting the Lord the next day. Often, I wanted something to happen to them so they would have a "wake up" moment to get back on track. Now I realize that was <u>my perspective</u> of how they should live their life; I wanted to see a changed person because of my own childish thought process. I am learning so much on my journey with God!

If we are on our journey of growth to becoming a mature man or woman of God…we are going to go through a process. And just like adolescent teenagers, it takes some people longer to mature than others. If you remember being a teenager, it can be super difficult to hold onto what we learn and know as the "right" thing to do. Even though we think we have it all together, it is at that point when we are actually struggling to keep the wheels from flying off, that we often push away our support system. Those moving through the 'adolescent years' in their faith often need the greatest support, as they are being bombarded with internal and external questions and challenged by worldly pressures.

"We must pray, not run away" during these times. This is where I could have completely lost my faith and my sense of being worthy of God. To be encouraged by unbelievers and condemned by believers at the same time is a terrible thing. And, this is where we seem to lose those young in their faith. If we can endure and overcome those experiences, we grow, ready to take on the next challenge with greater confidence, each time stepping away from our childish thoughts and actions.

And this can happen to a person pursuing God at any time in their life. <u>Spiritual age and calendar age are two different things, but the process can be almost identical.</u> Remember, age is just a number! The closer we draw near to God, our greatest supporter, the stronger we become on our own and in our faith. Don't push Him away and don't push away those who want to help you grow your faith as a Christian!

Ponder Point:

Step forward boldly in your journey as a child of God, faithful in prayer, growing in your actions, understandings and thoughts, so you can become a mature leader in this world to help those who are about to embark on their own journey of faith! All of the steps you take may help those yet to begin their own growing up with God!

A Place to Ponder and Pray

Let's Be Clear

Have you been wondering where your life is headed? Does the future seem clouded and the words muffled as you journey? Are you longing for a clearer understanding of what is going to happen next in your life?

In today's world, we want things to have clarity...to be crystal clear. We want clarity with greater resolution on our digital screens, higher sound quality from our audio systems, and anywhere/anytime access to what is happening (and what is supposed to happen). We also want to do more things at a distance, yet still have a seamless connection. We say we have too much going on to schedule true 'face-to-face' time. We want a life with "on demand" programming for everything, including our future.

The reality is that many of us have lost true clarity in our lives. We are in a hurry to get things done and we rush through the details. We are encouraged to demand immediate feedback. We have lost a sense of balance and executive functioning in how we use our gifted minds, God-given talents, and time.

Rather than focusing on ways to connect with one another, many people are choosing to pursue augmented realities. By definition, augmented means things are greater in value. Yet, we are actually diminishing the value of real-world human connections. We disconnect from real-life at the very moment we need to reconnect with one other and God in His world, not another form of reality!

Your ears shall hear a word behind you, saying, "This is the way, walk in it," whenever you turn to the right hand or whenever you turn to the left.
~ Isaiah 30:21

Throughout history, many have taken their focus away from the very thing that has the greatest clarity – God! Yet, again and again, He is patiently waiting, faithful, and ready to guide us, even when we seem blind to the world, He created for us.

Ponder Point:

You have a choice to re-balance your life…and you can make your choice right now! God's Word is true. It does not need to be called "augmented" to make it any greater! The Bible as written in its original form is vividly clear on what we can do to lead the life intended for us.

An Extraordinary Choice

No matter your circumstance, never forget you can make <u>one extraordinary choice</u>. You can choose to seek the kingdom of God. No one can deny you entrance based on your family's background, your past, your status, or your education. All you need to do is make a personal choice.

"But seek first the kingdom of God and all of his righteousness..."

~ Matthew 6:33

As we make choices in our lives, we need to be reminded that this verse does not just say to seek the kingdom of God, it actually states before you do anything, before you make any other choice..."Seek FIRST the kingdom of God and his righteousness".

Do you see the difference? It isn't just praying after you make a choice to seek God, but before you make a choice...go to Him for guidance and direction. Less worry will come your way. And as the second part of the verse states:

"…and all these things shall be added to you."
$\sim$ **Matthew 6:33**

Ponder Point:

Seeking God first is the best choice you will ever make. And with continual commitment to Him, you will find making other choices in life become easier.

Don't take my word for it. Follow God's Word! Go ahead…make a choice to <u>seek first</u> the kingdom of God and see what happens!!

What Do You Value?

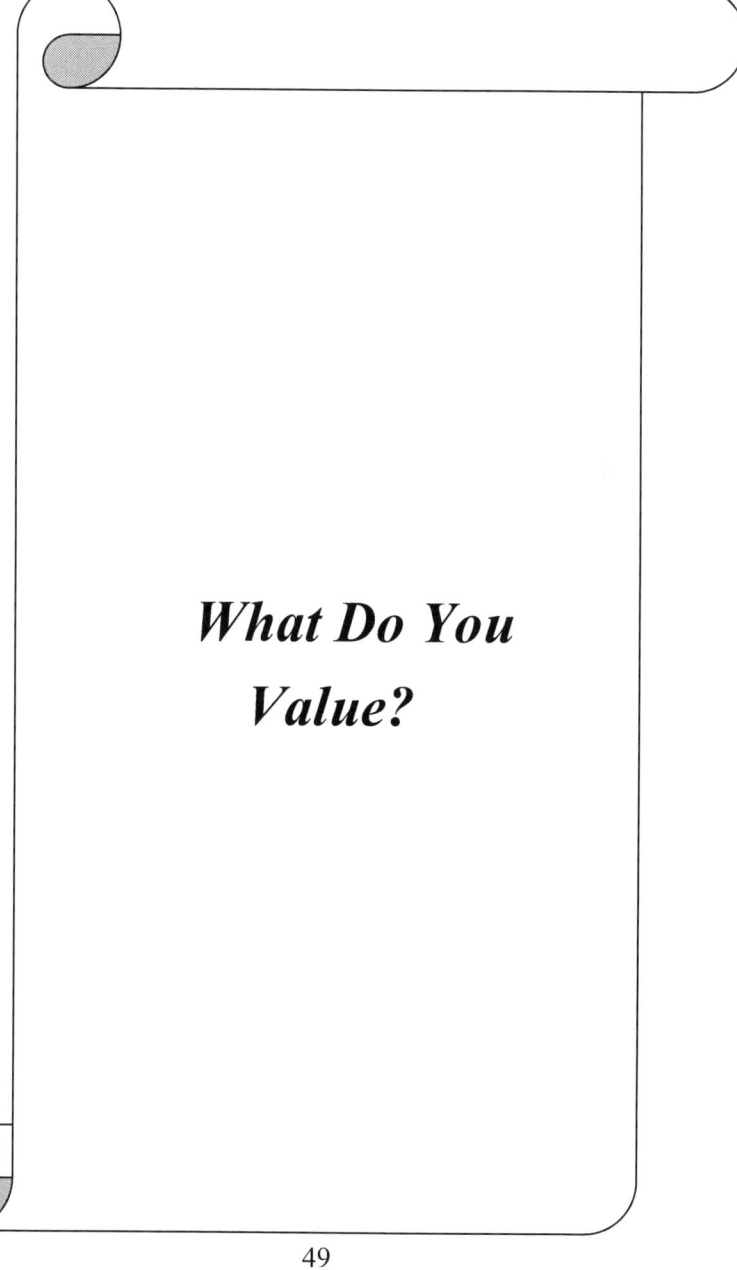

"...but lay up for yourselves treasures in heaven, where neither moth nor rust destroys and where thieves do not break in and steal. For where your treasure is, there your heart will be also."
~ Mathew 6:19-21

Superficial

We live in a superficial world. A world that often looks at things only on the surface. We seem content with knowing one another as hollow vessels. We have no desire to seek what makes someone whole. People believe what they see as real or true without looking more closely for details, evidence, and substance. Our society today, inspired by social media, provokes us to constantly check our self-worth based on 'likes' and acceptance by others. If we don't fit the identity of a mainstream group, we are "told" that we must be doing something wrong.

It is important we recognize we live in a fallen world. One where we must guard ourselves to not look only at the outward appearance of ourselves (or others), but rather to focus on the inward spirit expressed outwardly, the whole person. We need to check ourselves against God's guidelines, not those of our society and peers. As Jesus said:

"Blind Pharisee, first cleanse the inside of the cup and dish, that the outside of them may be clean also."
~ **Mathew 23:26**

Working from the inside out allows us to move beyond the superficial to the genuine grace of God and His planned purpose for us. It allows us to become all that God intends, not the world.

Ponder Point:

Do not let others define your appearance, purpose, or self-worth. Work on the details within your own heart, the very place others cannot see or judge you. Know your confidence comes from the grace of God, not from the superficial judgement of this world.

A "Why Me?" Attitude

I asked God, "Why me?" Have you ever uttered the same words? I must admit I have…not just once or twice, but more times than I ever should in my life! It may be human nature, but maybe it is time we change how we ask the question.

Do you ask *why me?* when things are not going well; when you feel defeated or cheated? I recently realized that we most often use these two words when things seem <u>nearly</u> impossible or unfair. It is often during a time of anger and resentment of our current circumstance. (I am not proud to say it, but it is true.) Instead, <u>could we, should we ask</u> *why me?* with appreciation and astonishment. What if each event has possibility and purpose beyond that moment? What if the situation just requires patience on our part to unveil its true blessing?

The more we search for our authentic self, the more we will recognize how our perspective and attitude about each event in our lives makes the biggest difference.

"Keep your heart with all diligence, for out of it springs the issues of life."

~ **Proverbs 4:23**

Ponder Point:

What is your perspective on the circumstances that surround your life? How do you ask the question *why me?* when things happen to you? Keep in mind the power of having an attitude of gratitude!

God's Way

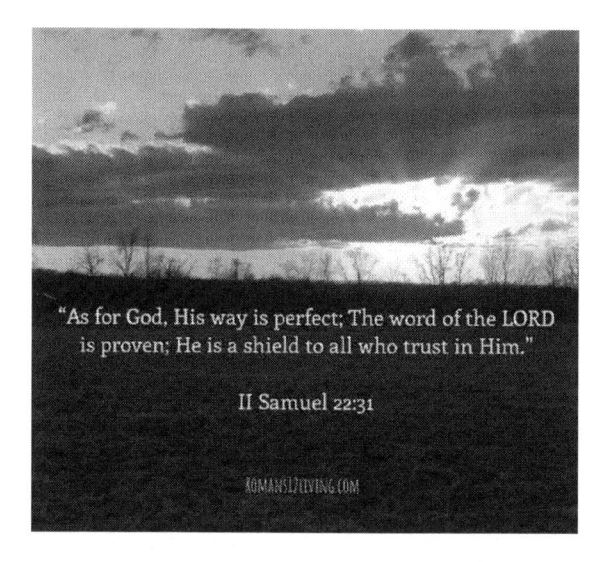

> "As for God, His way is perfect; The word of the LORD is proven; He is a shield to all who trust in Him."
>
> II Samuel 22:31

Integrity. Trust. Faith. Confidence. Commitment. Strength. If you can find these traits in a person, a group, or an organization, you should value it. Find a great place to grow in faith! When relationships (personal and professional) are high-functioning and successful, you seem to find these characteristics.

We are not perfect, but we can set a goal to follow God's Word and Way each day. We can choose to embody these traits in our relationships. Just as God wants us to build our lives with integrity and a trust to do what is right and in the best interest of all, we must have a faith and confidence in what is yet to come. We are all a work in progress, but God's word is proven. He will shield us and be our foundation.

"For who is God, except the Lord? And who is a rock, except our God?"

~ 2 Samuel 22:32

Ponder Point:

1. God's Way is perfect, even in our imperfect world. His words are proven throughout history and His love is never-ending. His Way is perfect, and He will guide us if we trust Him! God's Way is the way of integrity, trust, faith, confidence, commitment, and strength! Will you follow His Way?

Time or Money?

Time or money? Both things are necessary in our lives today and it seems there is never enough of either one to meet our needs <u>and wants</u>! Do you value one more than the other? God allows us to make choices. He provides us with all that we need, but we often overextend ourselves desiring things we want.

Even as you read this, are you contemplating the next step you want to take in your life? Do you think it is one that will give you an opportunity of greater freedom with time and money? Is it wrong for you to pursue a new venture? How can you be sure God is with you? Pray, serve God, and intently listen for His voice. No longer chase after things that cause you to be imbalanced in your mind, body, and spirit.

"No one can serve two masters. Either you will hate the one and love the other, or you will be devoted to the one and despise the other. You cannot serve both God and money."

~ **Matthew 6:24**

Gain freedom of yourself by serving God with your talents.

Ponder Point:

Have you ever thought about what is more important to you: time or money? Is it something you would like to change, but just do not know what to do? PRAY! Pray to God for guidance and listen to His voice, even if it means changes those things you may want. It takes time, but it is a wonderful gift to serve God in all you do!

Trust and Obey

Do you pay attention to the lyrics of songs? Music is storytelling, and church hymns are incredible faith stories that most people memorize, but never really take the time to study.

One song that really hit home for me is the old hymn "Trust and Obey" by John H. Stammis. Check it out here:

https://library.timelesstruths.org/music/Trust_and_Obey/

As you listen to it and look over the lyrics, you will find some amazing insights about your own potential. We have been called to a purpose beyond anything we might ever imagine! Opportunities and challenges are steps from where we were, to where we are now, to where we eventually will be…all on God's time.

We triumph and savor our moments of jubilation and opportunity. We struggle and question our life challenges. Yet, we must remember, nothing is possible <u>without</u> our glorious God.

Ponder Point:

Our role is not to understand, but rather to trust and obey. Today (and every day), make the decision to give your life, your talents, your struggles to God. We are here to purposefully serve as He desires! What an amazing journey awaits!

Gains and Losses

Nothing ventured, nothing gained! Yet each day, millions of people wake up concerned about losing what they have acquired rather than focusing on what matters most…gaining a relationship with God and other believers. Today's world is money-driven and status-stacked!

We are encouraged to be the best employee at work (sometimes even at the expense of others), so we can receive special recognition and monetary rewards for our efforts. Some people are told to marry for money, not love. And others believe worth is measured only in material things.

"He covets greedily all day long, But the righteous gives and does not spare."
~ Proverbs 21:26

People feel the need to show their status to others…often! Social media has made this even more prevalent, as our posts are now labeled as *status updates*.

We may have figured out ways to gain more 'stuff', but we need to weigh those things against what is lost. Are we losing our compassion for others, our patience with those in need, and our recognition of the small details that make our world and lives so uniquely diverse?

Ponder Point:

Are we missing the most profound moments in our lives just to gain more money and status? Are we losing ourselves? What about gaining eternal life through Jesus Christ?

Grounded

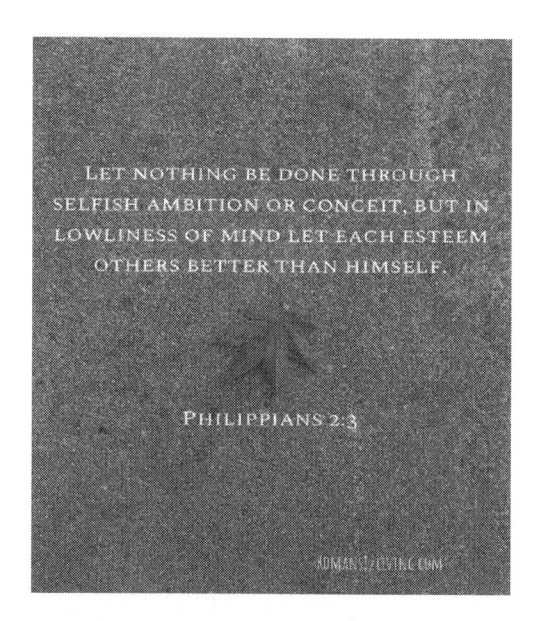

> LET NOTHING BE DONE THROUGH SELFISH AMBITION OR CONCEIT, BUT IN LOWLINESS OF MIND LET EACH ESTEEM OTHERS BETTER THAN HIMSELF.
>
> PHILIPPIANS 2:3

What are you known for? Are you humble or conceited? Are you selfless or selfish? Do you recognize those who helped open doors for you? Do you consciously look for ways to make a difference in the lives of others…without them knowing?

Being blessed with incredible people has helped open doors as I found my way in life, both professionally and personally. One of my most influential mentors told me, "I can get you to the plate, but you have to swing." Even then, he provided me with 'batting practice' tips, much like a baseball coach. Coaching me, encouraging me, building confidence in me, providing constructive criticism, and most importantly, keeping me grounded.

He warned me about others who used selfish or unscrupulous strategies to gain attention and status. He said I would encounter and have to deal with their direct attack on my integrity because those who are 'authentic' make those who are "fake" clearly obvious to others. Their moments in the sun are short-lived once others discover their conceited ways. Ultimately, it is better to <u>not</u> gain something if it is through devious means, but rather to earn something through authentic ambition.

Be authentic in the sense that you have no selfish ambition or conceit. Raise others up without expectation, even if it means you need to work harder. Use your experiences to help others, including sharing your mistakes. As you do these things, you will realize that an inner joy comes to your heart that <u>no one</u> can take away. You see, taking care of one another, especially other Christians, is all part of God's plan for us.

"And let us not grow weary while doing good, for in due season we shall reap if we do not lose heart. Therefore, as we have opportunity, let us do good to all, especially to those who are of the household of faith."
~ **Galatians 6:9-10**

The Best is Yet to Come

I remember my mother always telling me that high school was not going to be the high point in my life. Of course, having not experienced life beyond that time as a teenager made me disbelieve her. At that time, I felt as though I suffered through her strict rules and I gained little to no empathy for my whining. My friends (and their parents) felt sorry for me, wishing I could experience what they believed was the best part of life. For me, it seemed like the end of the world. Time passed and ageless saying "I told you so" was yet to be said again. The best was truly yet to come.

Good things happened. I found a fantastic job, a wonderful husband, and was blessed with beautiful, healthy babies. But, along with those happy times also came suffering.

As an adult, suffering takes on a different meaning. Losing loved ones, watching people agonize in their own pain, being pushed away by someone you truly care about as they make unhealthy choices. Isn't it interesting how our perspective changes as we experience life? I believe the same holds true for our experience with God's Word.

"For I consider that the sufferings of this present time are not worthy to be compared with the glory which shall be revealed in us."

~ Romans 8:18

Ponder Point:

For those of us who already have a relationship with God, we may have difficulty understanding how others can live without God in their life. Yet, we must not forget our own disbeliefs and struggles before we experienced His grace. What were our lives like before we built a relationship with Him? How can we help those who have yet to find Him?

Serving Others, Serving God

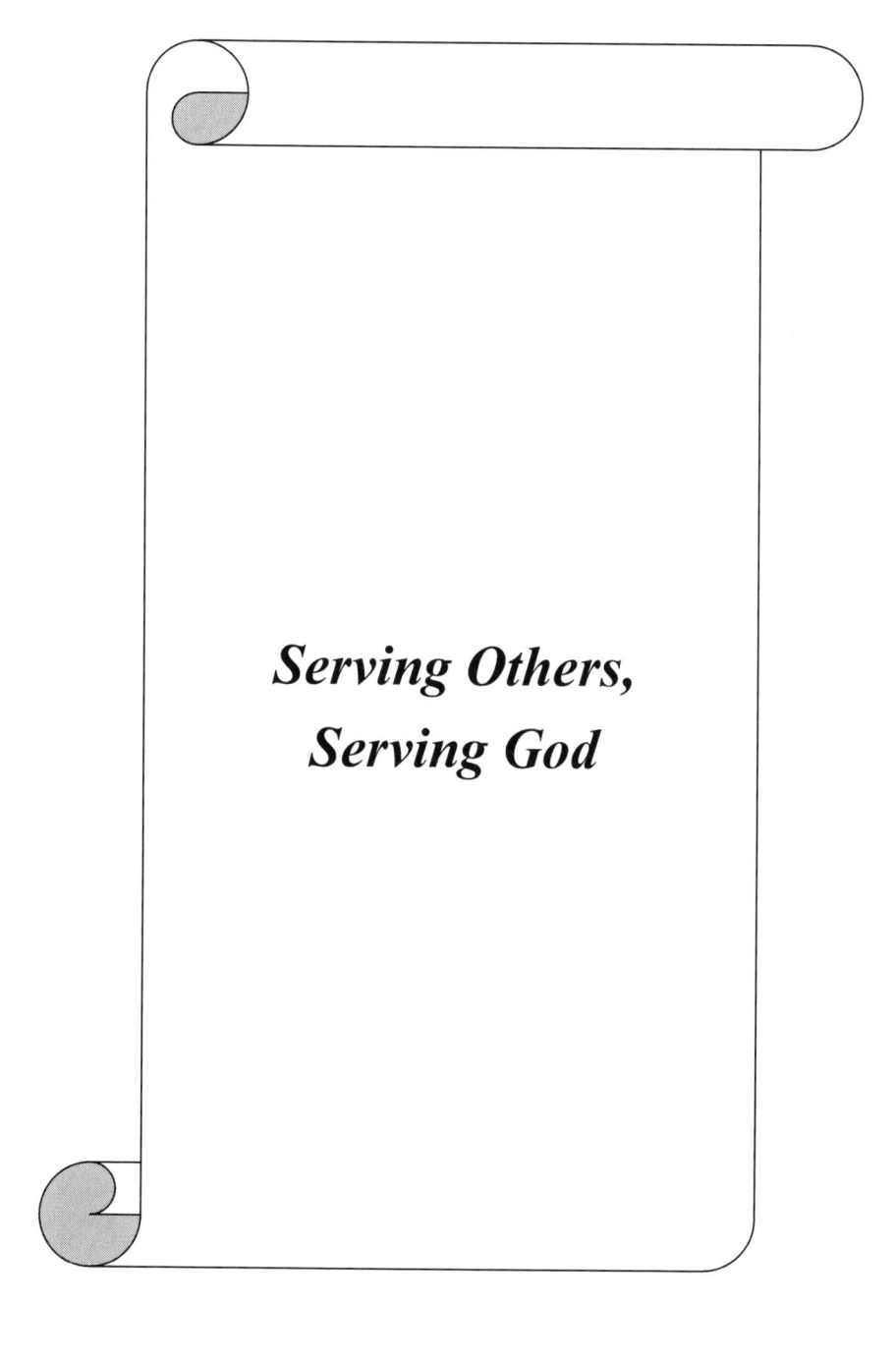

"For even the Son of Man did not come to be served, but to serve, and to give His life a ransom for many."

~ Mark 10:45

What is Service?

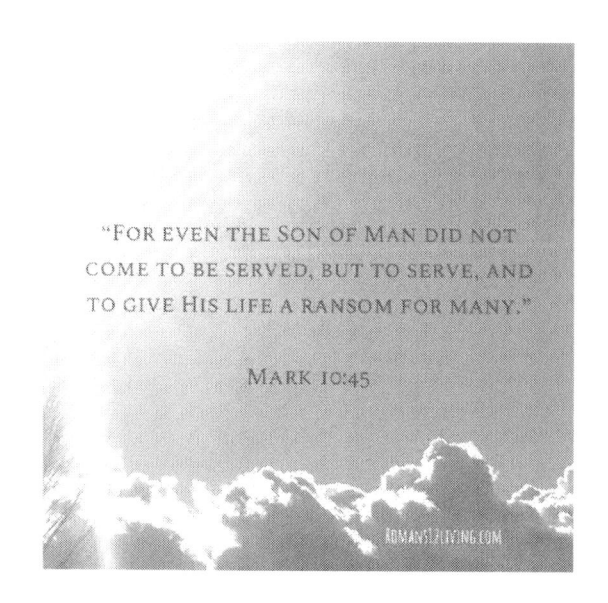

> "FOR EVEN THE SON OF MAN DID NOT COME TO BE SERVED, BUT TO SERVE, AND TO GIVE HIS LIFE A RANSOM FOR MANY."
>
> MARK 10:45

Each day we encounter examples of how others have served, including examples of service by people we will never meet! We may only think of the person right in front of us or a fancy name stamped on a business card. Look at the Scripture shared above and think about it. Our own small, daily decisions to serve others are absolutely needed and no less important. If everyone looked for ways to serve rather than to be served, the world would be incredibly different.

Think about it! In order for us to buy food at a restaurant or a store, there are people involved in getting that product to the point where we buy it. I mean lots of people (including those I will miss in this example). From the crop farmer who planted the lettuce, to the livestock farmer who birthed the calf...from the crop laborer who cared for the produce and the farm hand who cared for the livestock to make sure it was given the best conditions to grow...to the worker who harvested the crop for your choice produce and the truck driver who drove hundreds of miles delivering the goods; they all are serving a purpose beyond what we see in the end. Even the food buyer/supplier who purchased your products and the kitchen worker (or shelf stocker) who made it available for you, we need to recognize they are "hands-on" serving others.

Wow, there are lots of hands serving us! We may pay the cashier or the wait staff, but service begins in a place we often don't recognize at all. It's a "first step effort" by people who don't expect any recognition from the final consumer, yet they do their job...and they do it well!

We are called to serve...so decide to do the best job possible. I am sure you do something each day that goes unrecognized; just realize, without your service, the world would not be the same. Sure, maybe someone else could step in to complete your job, but each of us serves in some capacity that no one else could do exactly the same way.

Your call to serve is uniquely identified just for you. No matter if your service is recognized or hidden, it is important. To serve others extends beyond those you meet face-to-face! You have value and worth because you make a decision to serve. Serve and do great things!

A Place to Ponder and Pray

Fulfilling A Purpose

What is your most important job? Is it personal, professional, spiritual? Do you feel like you are living out your purpose and following the will of God? There are times when life is difficult, but remember what Jesus' said He was to do when questioned about His purpose.

Jesus said to them, "My food is to do the will of Him who sent me, and to finish His work."
~ **John 4:34**

How would you feel if God told you He had the same expectations for you as He did for Jesus? Jesus lived off the will of God as food. He was nourished by God to finish God's work. Nourishment is necessary for good health and condition. God provided for Jesus to have what He needed to complete His job, just as He does for us.

Each of us has a purpose! Personally, my health derailed my career, along with what I thought was my purpose in life as an educator. But, is it possible that God has an even greater purpose for me? Could everything I have done just been steppingstones to prepare me for His plan to fulfill His will? Or was I completely off course until now and He is closely guiding me on the right path? Joy comes from following His purpose. I need to continue to trust that He is in control, as I follow what He has planned for me. It may not financially provide as much money as my earlier job, but what is truly important in life? We must seek our purpose at all costs.

Ponder Point:

If you have doubts about what God intends for you to do or you are not able to trust His plans for you because of your finances, you are not alone. Many people have doubt in following the will of God and losing financial stability. Remember, God says He will provide for those things that finish His work. It may not be for all of our lavish wants, but He will fulfill our needs.

Be A Bridge Builder

Bridges are one of the most important physical structures we use in our lives. We likely take bridges for granted, especially if they are sturdy and we trust them from past experience. We don't even think twice when we cross over them. What makes a bridge so important in our lives? What purpose do bridges serve?

Bridges are used to connect places that would not be attainable due to physical obstacles; they provide a safe passage from point A to point B. There are many different designs of bridges, yet they all serve the same purpose. From simple steppingstones to suspension bridges they all accomplish the same goal. Each may function a bit differently due to terrain, materials, and available resources. Each one must pass a test of durability and reliability, even in the harshest environments.

Each one of us can be a bridge builder for others. We can mentor someone as they navigate how to get from point A to point B. Whether you are young or old, single or married, a parent or not, you are called to build bridges for others. Do not worry about the right materials. Use God's Word and think about what Jesus would do.

If you are alone without a mentor, work hard at building a bridge that will support both sides of your own journey. Remember your point A, as it is where your journey begins, but don't let it hold you back. As long as you build a sturdy bridge and don't burn it down as you cross over it, you will have the opportunity to return to help mentor others across the same bridge with a similar journey. We become the bridge maintenance crew, using God's Word to sustain the bridge for future generations.

Ponder Point:

Where are you in your journey with growing as a Christian? No matter if you are just finding your way across the bridge for the first time or you have years of experience mentoring others, remember the key elements of a bridge. It connects you to the next place in your life's journey. Even if the bridge moves a bit as you cross, know that durability and reliability need some flexibility to be sustainable. Once you are able to do so, become a bridge builder for others using the Word of God!

A Heart for God

It takes heart! Make a decision to work hard at whatever happens today, persevere through the difficulties, and pray during uncertain times. Praise God for your accomplishments. Working at your job, taking care of your family, completing schoolwork or chores, helping someone in need, managing life and caring for yourself; all of these show you have a lot going on each day. When the going gets tough, keep doing what is right! As this verse is written,

"And whatever you do, do it heartily <u>as to the Lord and not to men.</u>"
~ **Colossians 3:23**

What you do <u>should not be done</u> to impress the rest of the world. Sure, it feels awesome to be recognized by others for your talents and accomplishments. Appreciation and accolades can go a long way if you pursue what most people define as success. Make Godly choices, not earthly ones. But, most importantly, the real take away from today's verse is that whatever you do, do it with a heart for God. Do not continue to sin. Choose goodness and purity.

Ponder Point:

If we only seek approval from others, we are deeply missing the mark. We need to do everything with an open heart, focusing on what is right and good with God. We may fall short, but unlike the people around us, who have their own set of expectations for a job well done and short-lived success, God knows we are not perfect. He just wants us to do everything with a heart for Him and we will gain eternal approval in Heaven! Have a heart for the Lord! God bless you.

Guide on the Side

Does decision-making become easier as we grow older and wiser? Are we more at ease with the outcome or more trusting of our choices? Do we find ourselves thinking about what might happen…or are we trusting God's plan no matter what happens? Do we live in fear or in anticipation?

If you are reading this and you are a teenager, you may feel overwhelmed. Decisions have high stakes and you may feel as though you have less Godly support when making earthly decisions at a young age. It is true that lots of people are examining what teenagers do wrong, yet many of those same people are criticizing rather than mentoring and modeling what it means to do something right! We all need to work together to guide others through life choices. It does not mean we make other people's decisions, but we can talk about what it means to make good choices. What exactly does that mean?

- It means sharing a variety of ideas without telling someone exactly what to do.

- It means mentoring and encouraging others to think with perspective from a difficult viewpoint.
- It means giving opportunities for questions to be asked without personal judgment.
- It means guiding others based on Christian choices, not our own ideals! Interventions may be necessary.
- It means guiding others to not be anxious and worry, but rather to pray and request help from God. (Philippians 4:6)

Ponder Point:

Guiding others means we provide insight into choices with possible solutions and possible consequences; it's about having others think about the pros and cons for their choices based on Biblical principles.

"A man's heart plans his way, but the Lord directs his steps."

~ Proverbs 16:9

God is the one who says we shall lay our own paths and He will direct our steps. I need to fulfill my calling as a guide on the side; <u>no one is to take God's place.</u> Life experiences are important steps for each Christian to build faith and trust with God! I encourage you to find at least one way to be that important guide for someone you meet today.

Sharing with Others

Sharing is something we are often taught as young children. "It is better to give than to receive, so share what you have!" Yet, we seem to desire to share less as we acquire more things in life. Growing up, I had all that I truly needed, yet I was told to cherish my possessions and protect them from any possible harm, as if they were irreplaceable. I even had toys given to me that were not to be played with, but rather only looked at from a safe distance.

As a young adult, I had no real desire to share my hard-earned possessions. I told myself it was my fear and inability to replace the items due to cost, but I now realize I was selfish. I believed that because I worked so hard to earn them, I could not take the risk of allowing anyone else to use them. I justified that belief by telling myself I earned them <u>just for me</u>. What a sad statement. I now realize God blesses us to share, not hoard.

Reading a passage from the Bible, known by many as the *Parable of the Talents* (Matthew 25:14-29), is what led to this epiphany for me. This parable is telling us we have been entrusted with God's possessions and we are expected to make wise use of them. Our possessions are all gifts from God to be shared with others. They are not solely ours and they weren't given just for us to enjoy. (This includes our time and talents, not just stuff.) We are entrusted with each thing to glorify God and provide support for His Kingdom!

What a change of perspective this reading has given me. Will it possibly be a struggle to follow God's purpose with our possessions? Absolutely! Ask God to guide you. Give willingly and you will receive abundantly.

"But do not forget to do good and to share, for with such sacrifices God is well pleased."
~ Hebrews 13:16

Ponder Point:

What has God entrusted you to share with others? It may be a talent, your time, or your possessions. Can you make the decision to share with others today? Remember, everything we have God first shared with us! Trust in Him!

Walk the Walk

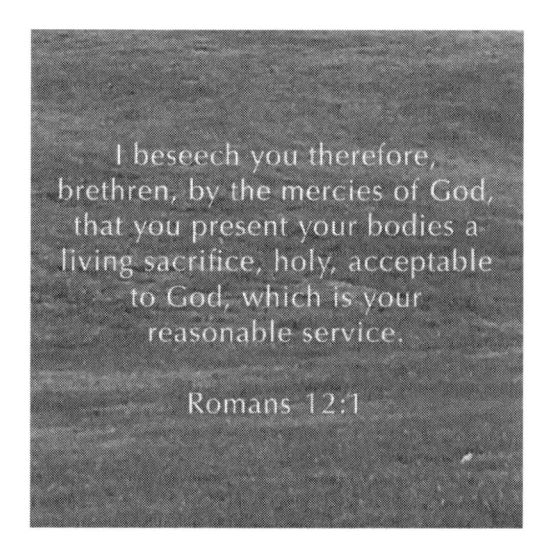

> I beseech you therefore, brethren, by the mercies of God, that you present your bodies a living sacrifice, holy, acceptable to God, which is your reasonable service.
>
> Romans 12:1

Promise yourself to make time to read Romans 12! It is the heart of my blog, *Romans 12 Living.* The book of Romans, Chapter 12 focuses on us and our decisions! It is a reminder for us to faithfully serve Him. What does it mean to "present yourself a living sacrifice" not by what we say, but by what we do? What about the words "reasonable service"? What is considered reasonable to God? What impact does Romans 12:1 (as seen above) have on your life?

Today's world has contorted so many words from the Bible that we have lost the true definition of their original and intended meaning. We often want to modernize words, change their meaning, and we use them out of context. We need to continue to walk the walk from the words God has provided us.

Unfortunately, the exact same thing holds true for so many people. <u>We have been contorted by this world and have lost our true meaning and God's intended purpose for us</u>. We are told we need to become "new-age" minded, more modern and less traditional, more liberal and less conservative. We become less and less of who God intends us to be, and we often don't realize it until we are lost. We then look at ourselves and we can't determine our purpose or identity.

How would you define yourself today? Are you striving to meet God's intended purpose for who you <u>are to be</u> in this world? Or are you following what someone else wants you to be for them?

Ponder Point:

As we serve God each day, remember the true Word He speaks through the Bible. We are not to serve this world's interpretation of His Word. We are to use ourselves as a living sacrifice to serve Him. Strive to live out His Word each day in your thoughts, words, and actions.

When in Doubt, Ask God

"But let him ask in faith, with no doubting, for he who doubts is like a wave of the sea driven and tossed by the wind."

~ James 1:6

You Are Not Alone

We all have felt alone at one time or another. It may have been physically alone, or it may have been a feeling of emotional, spiritual, or mental emptiness. Sometimes, we make choices that lead to loneliness, and other times, people choose to move themselves away from us. No matter what leads up to this sense of loneliness, take heart and know you are not truly alone. There are other people experiencing feelings just like yours.

God is with you! If you decide to stand for something you know is truthful and right, God stands with you. If you choose to say no to something that may be socially conforming but is ethically wrong, God stands with you. People, ones you will never meet, are making the same decision to stand up for Christ. We need to recognize those who seek spiritual authenticity.

The world is filled with lots of ways to connect, even at a distance. Follow *Romans 12 Living* blog, podcasts like *Walking Barefoot with the Bible* and *Why Balance Matters*, so reach out to others in your local community, and take time to 'people watch'. You will quickly discover those who are spiritually authentic by watching how they interact with others and themselves.

Take heart…

"Do not fear, for those who are with us are more than those who are with them."

~ **II Kings 6:16**

... you are not alone!

Choice Words

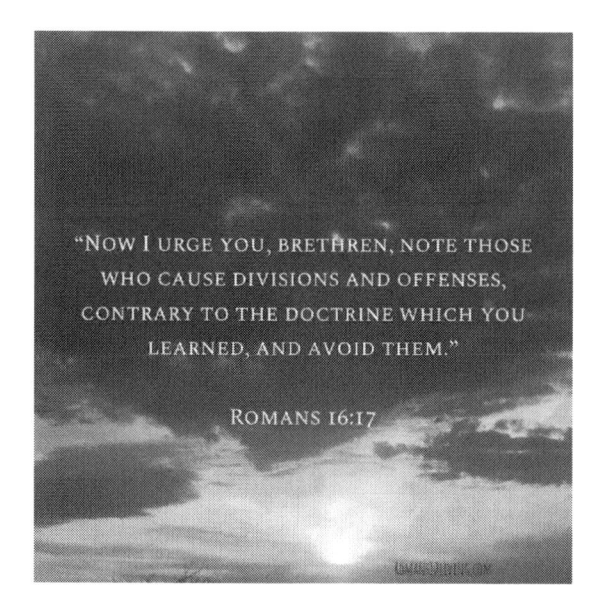

> "NOW I URGE YOU, BRETHREN, NOTE THOSE WHO CAUSE DIVISIONS AND OFFENSES, CONTRARY TO THE DOCTRINE WHICH YOU LEARNED, AND AVOID THEM."
>
> ROMANS 16:17

Do you ever find others want to argue just to create conflict? Be strong and resist; don't waste time on their deceitful plans. Acknowledge what is right and do not get caught in the tumultuous storm of their words. **Avoid arguments with divisive people**. They thrive on conflict and feel empowered with debate. (If you do choose to argue, be prepared to battle with God as your guide.)

Check out the Bible verse shared on the previous page, read over and reflect on its words. How does this verse influence your choice words? Do not allow others to attempt to turn you away from the teachings you learned from God's Word and commands. It may be difficult, but you must choose to do what is right, not what is easy!

"For those who are such do not serve our Lord Jesus Christ, but their own belly, and by smooth words and flattering speech deceive the hearts of the simple."
~ **Romans 16:18**

We need to be prepared for those smooth talkers, who may deceive our friends and family members. They attempt to influence us with flattering speech, yet they have ulterior motives. Do not get caught in their web of words!

Ponder Point:

Be prepared!
- Arm yourself with the Word of God
- Pray for strength and awareness
- Have your actions model as evidence of your faith!
- Follow God's teachings!

Have Courage

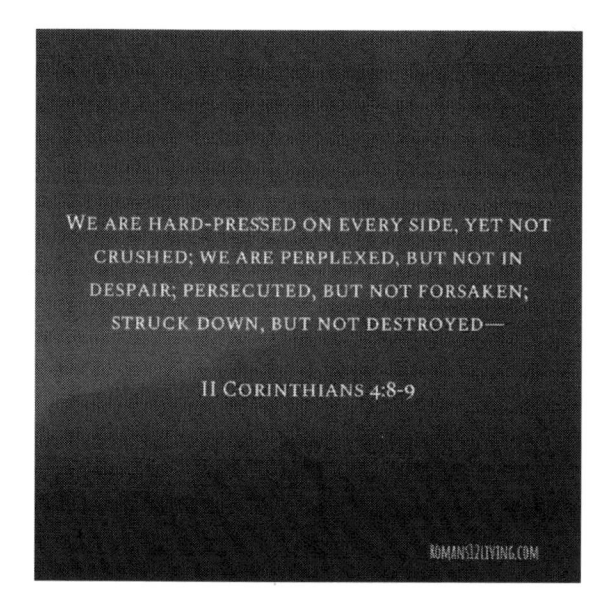

> WE ARE HARD-PRESSED ON EVERY SIDE, YET NOT CRUSHED; WE ARE PERPLEXED, BUT NOT IN DESPAIR; PERSECUTED, BUT NOT FORSAKEN; STRUCK DOWN, BUT NOT DESTROYED—
>
> II CORINTHIANS 4:8-9

It seems like we can turn any direction and the world is against those who follow Jesus Christ! Social media has influenced so many of us to turn away. It is a "blind leading the blind" movement! Do not be discouraged, rather have courage. Speak up, professing your faith in God, and encouraging others to do the same. This battle of oppression, perplexity, persecution, and pain have been ongoing since the Old Testament.

"We are hard-pressed on every side, yet not crushed; we are perplexed, but not in despair; persecuted, but not forsake; struck down, but not destroyed-"
~ **II Corinthians 4:8-9**

We may be pressed from all directions, but we have not been crushed! Yes, it may seem like we can't make a Godly decision without pressure from others. No matter what, stand strong against <u>social conformity</u>!

We may feel alienated by this world we live in today…the disturbing thoughts and irrational emotions of others, even as they defend their way to be true and rational. It seems so odd what they believe to be the 'way of the world'. Stand strong even as we are being persecuted for basing our lives and decisions on the Holy Bible. We must not quit or conform. We need to be <u>spiritually authentic</u>! We can and will find clarity with Christ. You are not alone.

Ponder Point:

Be steadfast in knowing that we are not forsaken for God is with us; he will never leave us. Find hope in His promises! Even through all of this, we will be attacked and struck down, but have COURAGE, for <u>we will not be destroyed</u>. We have eternal life awaiting us with our God!!

Attention, Please!

We all choose how we behave; our decisions become habits. A habit is defined as a regular tendency, one that is difficult to give up. Sometimes bad habits start as an action being used to gain attention. Like most bad habits, people choose to blame someone else for their own poor decisions.

Friends often have similar behaviors. We don't often pay attention to it, but we become like those we associate with, unless we guard our hearts. We often end up with the same bad habit; it may seem acceptable to have the habit when you hang out with certain people. Those people you consider to be your friends may even encourage you to not change your similar habits, because it empowers them to believe they are doing things "right". Perhaps, they had you change your ways from good to bad. Think for yourself, using God as your guide! Seek His attention, not the attention of others!

"While they promise them liberty, they themselves are slaves of corruption; for by whom a person is overcome, by him also he is brought into bondage."

~ 2 Peter 2:19

> Ponder Point:

I encourage you to pray for strength from God and seek His attention in place of that behavior that led you to a bad habit! Change your environment, change your focus, and see what you can do to get rid of that bad habit. It is amazing what you can accomplish with God! You may have to leave behind the bad influence of others, but God will guide you and protect you. What God wants for you, no one can stop!

Gut Feelings

"For when Gentiles, who do not have the law, by nature do the things in the law, these, although not having the law are a law to themselves, who show the work of the law <u>written in their hearts, their conscience also bearing witness</u>, and between themselves their thoughts accusing or else excusing them."
~ **Romans 2:14-15**

We all have made decisions and experienced events in our lives that have taken us to less than extraordinary places. I am talking about the ones with deep anxiety, gut-wrenching "this is not right" moments, and a few "Dear God, please get me out of this place" events. Bad decisions put us in tough situations.

If you look back at those experiences with an open mind, ask yourself:

1. Was I listening to God? (which I connect to my gut-feelings). If not, realize you went astray from His plan, yet through His amazing grace He redeemed you.

2. Have I learned from my experiences? Extreme Earthly events help us gain a clearer spiritual perspective of life here on Earth about right and wrong. Learning from sinful mistakes is what matters.

Ponder Point:

We each have our own 'gut-feeling' of what is right or wrong, what should be okay or not. I encourage you to listen to your gut and pray to God. When you get those unsettled feelings of concern, acknowledge them and reflect on what is happening around you. If you are anxious, do not make a rushed decision and act. Pray.

God wants us to make good decisions, but He also does not expect us to be perfect. Learn from your mistakes, do not repeat them, mentor others about making good decisions, read God's Word, and follow God's special purpose for you!

Be Prepared

"A prudent man foresees evil and hides himself; the simple pass on and are punished."
~ Proverbs 27:12

I read this verse and it connected to something I sometimes tell my children. "Prepare for the worst and plan for the best." It may sound negative, but that truly is not my goal. I tell them this because we need to take on the world with God by our side.

It is similar to packing an emergency kit for your car. You place all of the possible disaster/emergency items in that kit. You know how to use them, if needed! You learn what to avoid on your journey because you listen to others whom you trust. By being prudent, you follow God's Word.

By doing so, you can take a deep breath and be worry-free. You know you planned well for your journey and you have faith it will be okay. Why? Because you are prepared to handle whatever may happen. This does not mean you may not run into trouble, but you have your emergency kit, God's Word, readily available.

Ponder Point:

Being prepared does not mean you are in control; it simply means you are keeping your eyes open for evil, attempting to avoid it. God is with you wherever you journey. Keep the Bible nearby to help guide your way! Pray to God for guidance and protection!

Draw Near to God

"Draw near to God and He will draw near to you."
~ James 4:8

We all can feel lost at times! When you feel lost, abandoned and alone, draw near to God…pray, read the Bible, and find some quiet time to patiently listen for Him.

If you feel alone right now, take this time to talk with God and spend quality time listening to Him! Pray and connect with Him! You may not be able to make choices for others, but you can make this choice for yourself!

"Behold, I am with you and will keep you wherever you go, and will bring you back to this land; for I will not leave you until I have done what I have spoken to you."
~ Genesis 28:15

Ponder Point:

Remember, you cannot choose what other people say and do, you can only control what <u>you choose</u> to say and do.

A Place to Ponder and Pray

Faith and Hope

"Now faith is the substance of things hoped for, the evidence of things not seen!"
                                                      ~ **Hebrews 11:1**

Just when things seem to be getting better, we often have a setback. Sometimes, when we think we cannot handle anything else, we are even more overwhelmed.

Life is full of uncertainty. We must not lose faith in our awesome God. We need to have hope in what is yet to come. God is with each of us, including you. Pray to Him as you struggle with setbacks and ask Him for strength when you feel overwhelmed.

"But Jesus looked at them and said, "With men it is impossible, but not with God; for with God all things are possible."
                                                      ~ **Mark 10:27**

A Place to Ponder and Pray

My Refuge

The world can be harsh. Life is not always easy; we live in a fallen world. We face physical and mental struggles, sorrow, anger, loneliness, and pain. We may even feel like running away from ourselves because the pain seems intolerable. We MUST always remember God is our refuge. We <u>must run to Him</u>!

No matter how dismal the situation or horrific the pain, pray steadfastly to God! He is with you even when you feel alone! He will never forget you, and He will give you strength when you feel weak. He will give you security when you feel scared. He will give you peace when you are tormented.

"When you pass through the waters, I will be with you; And through the rivers, they shall not overflow you. When you walk through the fire, you shall not be burned, Nor shall the flame scorch you."

~ Isaiah 43:2

Just pray to Him with all your heart and have faith in what is yet to come. Realize we cannot control time; be patient and know God is with you.

Remember always…

"I will say of the LORD, "He is my refuge and my fortress; My God, in Him I will trust."
$\sim$ **Psalms 91:2**

Trust God, no matter what!

Time for a Relationship with God

"Therefore humble yourselves under the mighty hand of God, that He may exalt you in due time, casting all your care upon Him, for He cares for you."

~ 1 Peter 5:6

Our Life's Tapestry

Ornately decorated tapestries have been valued throughout history as they are picture stories of someone's life and family, their heritage in art. We may not have tapestries physically woven and hanging in our homes, but we do hang them in our minds. Each tapestry is our life story woven together by experiences and human relationships. Not all of our stories are wonderful, but our life's tapestry is a testimony of what we have experienced…the good, the bad, and the in-between. Yet, we are often so busy attempting to forget our past or planning the next moments in our future, we don't stop to take in where we are right now in weaving together our personal tapestry. We miss so many of our "here and now" moments because we are running from our "there and then" or focusing on "where and when".

Take time today to truly reflect and enjoy the interconnected tapestry of your life…with beautiful strands of many colors representing who you are in mind, body, and spirit.

Moments from your past will leap into the spotlight, providing you with a reflective perspective, one telling you to search for answers to questions you never even knew to ask until now. Be patient and forgiving. Think about your life's tapestry…are you weaving a tapestry you are happy with? What do you need to do to make a tapestry you are pleased with? Your work is not complete!

"The Lord shall preserve your going out and your coming in. From this time forth, and even forevermore."
~ **Psalms 121:8**

Ponder Point:

Promise yourself to take just a few moments right now to reflect on your life story. Look at the big picture and see what connections you find interwoven into your life's tapestry. Thank God for his love and patience with each thread in your tapestry of life, good or bad, recognizing its purpose. Focus on where are you today and where God wants you to be in the future.

Taking Care of Yourself

"...glorify God in your body."
                              ~ **1 Corinthians 6:20**

How well are you taking care of yourself? I mean by making healthy choices, not self-indulgent "in the moment" choices. A 'healthy you' makes you healthy for others. As we struggle to balance our family and job responsibilities, there might be very little time to really focus on self-care.

God created each of us for a specific purpose. You are blessed with a specific role that no one else can fulfill!! God also allows us free will with our time, hoping that we glorify Him in all we do. Are you taking care of your body? Do you nourish it with foods to keep it healthy? The Bible has numerous references to nuts, vegetables, fish, and lean meats. God did not create junk food. He created healthy foods, which we still have today.

Having the willpower to eat healthy is not easy. Temptation is everywhere. Even today, we will be tempted to eat and drink the very things we know are not healthy, some of which even make us feel sick. Why? We live in a fallen world. If we are tempted and choose to make unhealthy decisions, we cannot complete God's purpose.

What about taking care of your mind? What information do you seek to fill your mind with? Is it positive and informative? Or is it negative and unproductive? Ask God for knowledge and wisdom!

"If any of you lacks wisdom, let him ask of God, who gives to all liberally and without reproach, and it will be given to him."
~ James 1:5

Most importantly, how are you taking care of your spirit? Do you pray to God for guidance, strength, support, and forgiveness? Is there time set aside each day just for quiet reflection with Him?

"Then you will call upon Me and go and pray to Me, and I will listen to you."
~ Jeremiah 29:12

**You are stronger than any temptation
with God as your guide.**

"For you were bought at a price; therefore, glorify God in your body and in your spirit, which are God's."
~ 1 Corinthians 6:20

No Stone Unturned

I was recently talking with someone and I mentioned leaving 'no stone unturned' in my pursuit of wellness. It then hit me, like a ton of bricks.

As I began digging for more knowledge about my health, I pushed aside small stones of information to find larger ones with greater evidence. I even started chipping away at boulders of doubt from others to trust God. Just so you know, those boulders are the heaviest to overturn. (Maybe you feel the same thing, just in a different situation.) I was making little progress, feeling like I lost momentum and direction. The disbelief from others about what was making me ill was causing me to feel mentally defeated.

As tired and weak as my body was at that time, I knew I had to continue moving stones. There had to be an answer to what was happening to me. I truly believe God provided me with the needed strength. So, I continued (and continue) to dig deeper and leave no stone unturned in my pursuit of health.

The true beauty and grace that God provides make me realize that I am not only leaving no stone unturned with my physical self, but I am also pursuing and finding answers that are strengthening my spiritual self.

You see, the Bible mentions stones (rocks) numerous times in the Bible, as foundation and mountains. Recognize the need for patience in your life.

"Therefore thus says the Lord GOD: "Behold, I lay in Zion a stone for a foundation, A tried stone, a precious cornerstone, a sure foundation; Whoever believes will not act hastily."

~ Isaiah 28:16

God is my foundation: physically, mentally, and spiritually. Our salvation through Jesus Christ is what matters most. Leave no stone unturned. Seek answers through God. I was looking to regain my health and I regained something even greater…my spiritual self.

Ponder Point:

"Have you not even read this Scripture: 'The stone which the builders rejected Has become the chief cornerstone."

~ Mark 12:10

Waiting

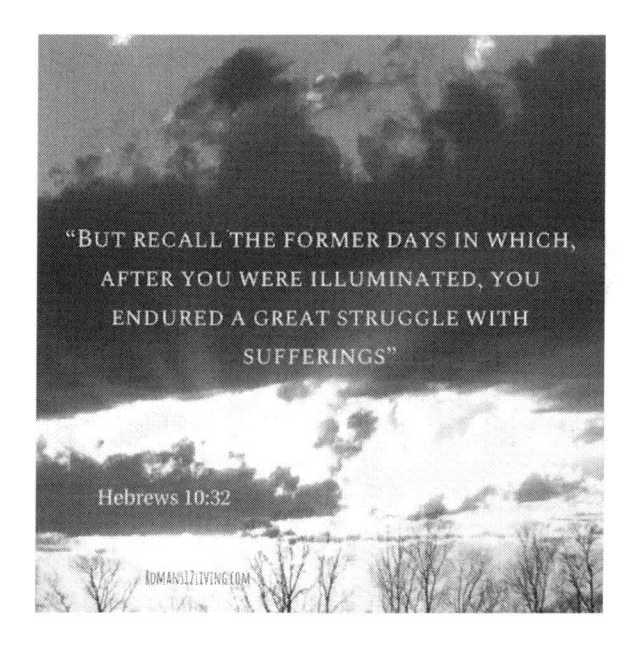

> "BUT RECALL THE FORMER DAYS IN WHICH, AFTER YOU WERE ILLUMINATED, YOU ENDURED A GREAT STRUGGLE WITH SUFFERINGS"
>
> Hebrews 10:32

'I'll be back in the high life again.'

I'm not sure if you ever heard someone say this, but I think it basically means you remember when things were going really well in your life and you seemed to have it all…or at least in that moment, it just felt great to be YOU!

People usually say this statement when they are NOT living those 'high-life' moments. It is when they are at a low point, a place of distress or fear…but they still have hope in what is yet to come. A hope that the 'high-life' will come again!

Have you experienced any 'high-life' events in your life? Perhaps you overlooked a few of them, not fully appreciating them? Honestly, God has blessed many of us beyond what others may only dream of in a lifetime. What an awesome God He is!

Nevertheless, low points in life are hard to understand. Have you ever felt led by God to a place you never imagined or followed a path where you did not know what was to happen next? Were you anxious?

My illness caused the loss of my professional identity. I had no clear purpose about what to do next with a ton of mental and physical hurdles blocking my way. You see, many things that came so easily to me became difficult. The skills I was once praised and rewarded for became impossible.

God has a <u>plan for every single thing in your life</u>! Seek to see His glory in action. Know everything has a reason, even as we struggle.

"Blessed is the man who endures temptation; for when he has been approved, he will receive the crown of life which the Lord has promised to those who love Him."
*~ **James 1:12***

Justified and Glorified

Justified! You are declared and made righteous in the sight of God because of your faith.

This means no matter what happens in your life, you do not need to worry about your relationship with God. You can have peace with God because of Jesus Christ.

Glorified! Even beyond being justified, God also glorifies you.

"Moreover, whom He predestined, these He also called; whom He called, these He also justified; and whom He justified, these He also glorified."
~ Romans 8:30

God has big plans for you; plans beyond anything you might think is possible. You may be in a place right now that is less than ideal. Don't worry, God will meet you where you are.

Pray for strength. He has plans for you to glorify His kingdom. Never doubt the timeline of God or His power! Be blessed in mind and body knowing you are justified and glorified through Jesus Christ!

A Place to Ponder and Pray

The Best Day

What would be the perfect day for you? A day off work with full pay? Time spent at a spa or on a hike? No dishes to wash or dinner to cook? Time spent with your favorite person? A warm, sunny spot to sit and relax? All of these examples seem to exhibit two common ideas – peace and happiness.

We often daydream about the perfect day to find that it may never truly meet our expectations. Perfection is not 100% attainable here on Earth. Of course, we may find people who always have a great attitude and outlook on life. They allow for minor flaws to fade away and often have many seemingly perfect days. We should aspire to have an attitude of gratitude, even with little imperfections.

"Come to me, all you who labor and are heavy laden, and I will give you rest."
                                                              ~ **Matthew 11:28**

The grace of God provides us peace in an imperfect world. We must seek a positive attitude to allow this grace to enter our lives. We are always given the freedom to choose a negative or a positive attitude. Keep this in mind whenever you think of your perfect day!

Ponder Point:

What brings you peace and happiness? God wants us to find peace and joy. Look at each imperfect day with open eyes, ears, and a heart of gratitude. Ask God to help you as you change your attitude to one of gratitude!

Seek Good in All

"He who earnestly seeks good finds favor, but trouble will come to him who seeks evil."
>> **~ Proverbs 11:27**

In a world that seems to focus on evil and its desire to fracture any semblance of good, dig deep and respond with an attitude of appreciation and seek goodness. Steer away from trouble.

"See that no one renders evil for evil to anyone, but always pursue what is good both for yourselves and for all. Rejoice always, pray without ceasing, in everything give thanks; for this is the will of God in Christ Jesus for you."
>> **~ I Thessalonians 5:15-18**

Choose to do the following:
- Look for the good in every situation.
- Search for the silver lining with every experience.
- Find something amazing about every person you meet (and share it with them).

A Place to Ponder and Pray

Leave a Legacy

"Let nothing be done through selfish ambition or conceit, but in lowliness of mind let each esteem others better than himself."
~ **Philippians 2:3**

God wants us to help one another! He created each of us with special talents for a purpose beyond what we may see on a superficial level. Sadly, some people never look beyond that superficial level to see their ambitions are not to be for their own glory, but rather God's glory. God does amazing things in our lives. Unfortunately, there are many successful people who continue to use their time in the spotlight to promote themselves or ungodly platforms rather than promoting God's goodness through sharing their love for Him and helping others. What if they chose to <u>not</u> stand on a podium with selfish pride and conceit, but use that moment as a platform to springboard the success of those less fortunate or struggling in life? What if they decided to inspire and lift up those around them using the salvation of Jesus Christ?

There are so many people just waiting for someone to care about them, to be a mentor, to open a door of opportunity. They just want a chance to be nurtured and given an opportunity to grow their Godly gifts. Each of us has a choice. We can inspire others to reach their potential or we can manipulate the situation to make ourselves feel superior and others inferior.

Don't allow your blessings to become your conceit! Encourage and lift others up; choose to make a positive difference in the lives of others. Be humble!

Do you ever have other people telling you about how amazing they are and all of the things they have done? We rarely hear those people share the struggles and challenges in their lives; they don't share their mistakes and missteps. They often paint a picture showcasing their accomplishments and giving credit only to themselves.

Your greatest glory in life does not happen in the spotlight; it happens in the shadows of those you inspire, encourage, and guide! It is a legacy you choose to live for others rather than a fleeting moment in time you choose to live for your own glory!

Let your light shine before men that they may see your good works and glorify your Father in heaven."
                                              ~ Matthew 5:16

Ponder Point:

Just remember, no matter how many accomplishments, accolades, and awards you may gain, choose to be humble and let others tell your story. Be a legacy builder for others. Let your light shine!

A Place to Ponder and Pray

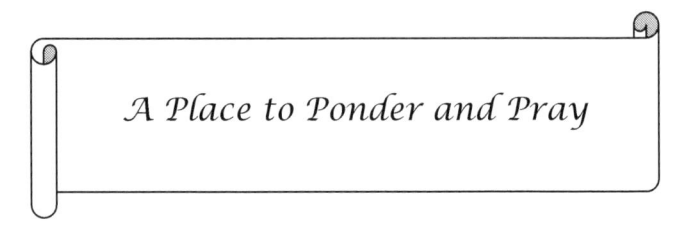

If interested, please contact me about speaking with your group or developing educational resources to support your goals.

Blessings,

Rebecca

dr.rebecca.speelman@gmail.com

romans12living.com

www.whybalancematters.com

Made in the USA
Middletown, DE
30 April 2021